POP CULTURE PERSONALITIES

ROAR!

ENTERTAINER

JOHN CENA

by Alex Hall

BEARPORT PUBLISHING

Roar! Books, an imprint of Bearport Publishing by FlutterBee

Credits
Images are courtesy of Shutterstock.com and Alamy, unless otherwise stated. Cover – Kathy Hutchins, vladwel, Kingwardobe, M_Videous, Dzm1try, rudidwihantoro, shahana48, Rvector, Vectomart, Vlad Ra27, robuart. 4–5 – New Africa, Tinseltown. 6–7 – Everett Collection, Stock Rocket. 8–9 – Little Vignettes Photo, agil73. 10–11 – Shamsuddin Muhammad, CC BY 2.0, via Wikimedia Commons, Mmsnapplez, CC BY-SA 4.0, via Wikimedia Commons, ZUMA Press Inc. 12–13 – quiggyt4. 14–15 – Sam Aronov, Gage Skidmore from Peoria, AZ, United States of America, CC BY-SA 2.0, via Wikimedia Commons, Allstar Picture Library Ltd. 16–17 – Randall Chancellor from Austin, TX, CC BYSA 2.0, via Wikimedia Commons, felipe bascuñan, CC BY-SA 2.0, via Wikimedia Commons. 18–19 – DFree, Gage Skidmore from Peoria, AZ, United States of America, CC BY-SA 2.0, via Wikimedia Commons. 20–21 – lev radin. 22–23 – lev radin, Sam Aronov.

Bearport Publishing Company Product Development Team
Kayla Eggert, Theresa Emminizer, Kim Jones, Allison Juda, Cole Nelson, Naomi Reich, Steve Scheluchin, Tiana Tran

Library of Congress Cataloging-in-Publication Data is available at www.loc.gov or upon request from the publisher.

ISBN: 979-8-89577-830-2 (hardcover)
ISBN: 979-8-89577-838-8 (ebook)

For more information, write to Bearport Publishing, 3500 American Blvd W, Suite 150, Bloomington, MN 55431. Printed in the United States of America.

CONTENTS

POP CULTURE PERSONALITY

Some fans race to see his movies. Others love to watch him wrestle in the ring. But who is John Cena?

John Cena is a professional wrestler and actor. He is one of world's biggest **entertainers.**

CHILDHOOD

John was born in Massachusetts on April 23, 1977. His father was a wrestling **announcer.**

John and his brothers loved wrestling as children. Together, they made championship belts out of cardboard.

EARLY CAREER

John moved to California in 1998. He started to work out to become a **bodybuilder**. Then, he decided to become a professional wrestler.

Wrestlers train to do their job safely. Once he had trained enough, John started wrestling in small **flea markets.**

WORLD WRESTLING FEDERATION

In 2000, John started wrestling for the World Wrestling Federation (WWF). His first matches were not major events.

In 2001, John Cena signed a contract with the WWF. His first competition for TV finally happened in 2002.

WWE CHAMPION

The WWF changed its name to the WWE in 2002. John continued working his way to the top.

In 2005, he became the WWE champion. He has since won the champion belt more times than anyone else.

FEUDS

John has faced off against some of the biggest stars in wrestling, such as Randy Orton and CM Punk.

The Rock was one of his biggest rivals. They starred in the WrestleMania main event two years in a row.

WRESTLING SUPERSTAR

John took on bigger and bigger stages. He won many titles both alone and in tag team matches.

Some people say he is the best wrestler of all time. But that isn't all he does.

ACTING

In 2000, John started acting in movies. He is an action star. And he acts in comedies.

John also acts on TV shows. He has even hosted challenge shows, such as *Wipeout*.

CHARITY WORK

John spends a lot of time helping others. He has used his fame to support many **charities.**

John has granted more than 650 wishes for ill children through the Make-A-Wish Foundation. This is hundreds more than anybody else.

WHAT IS NEXT?

John Cena went from bodybuilding to wrestling and starring in movies. He works hard at everything he does.

This wrestler and actor has become one of the biggest stars in entertainment. What is your favorite thing about John Cena?

GLOSSARY

announcer a person who describes and comments on the action in a sports event

bodybuilder a person who tries to gain a lot of muscle and competes with others doing the same

charities organizations that help those in need

entertainers people who perform to amuse others

flea markets outdoor markets, often selling vintage or second-hand goods

INDEX